"Do to others as you would have them do to you."
—Matthew 7:12

"A people without knowledge of their ancestral history are like a tree without roots." —A.F.S.

"Only by knowing about slavery can one prevent it from happening again." —C.C.

"Beyond the Legacy of Slavery is enlightening, inspiring, motivating, provoking, entertaining and enjoyable. Once I started reading the book, I couldn't wait to finish it." —G.W.

"His ancestral and anointed name of Morlai Koroma, interpreted as 'the respected friend of God,' reflect the life and times of Bertram L. Charles, Esquire." —M.H.C.

"From the story of the night of enslavement, death, pain, misery, tears and oppression to the day of emancipation, bliss and reunion of the ancestors' physical and spiritual presence." —E.W.S.

"The grace of God played the supreme role in the life story of Bertram L. Charles. His narrative not only offers a uniquely personal experience but also tenders a universal account of the evils of slavery and the promise of hope in overcoming its tragedies." —O.M.H.

"The racism, injustice and inequality of the Jena 6 case of Jena, Louisiana, remind us that the poison of the legacy of slavery must be purged and eradicated." —B.L. Herbert

BEYOND *the* LEGACY *of* SLAVERY

From St. Kitts to Sierra Leone

BERTRAM L. CHARLES

Except where otherwise indicated all Scripture quotations are taken from the King James Version of the Bible.

Verses marked AMP are taken from The Amplified Bible, Old Testament, Copyright © 1965 and 1987 by The Zondervan Corporation, and from The Amplified Bible, New Testament, Copyright © 1954, 1958, 1987 by The Lockman Foundation. Used by permission.

Publisher's Cataloging-in-Publication Data
(Provided by Cassidy Cataloguing Services, Inc.)

Charles, Bertram L.

    Beyond the legacy of slavery : from St. Kitts to Sierra Leone /
    Bertram L. Charles and Morlai Koroma. -- 1st ed. -- Christiansted,
    U.S. Virgin Islands : Bertram L. Charles, 2008.

    p. ; cm.

    ISBN: 978-1-933150-14-7
    Includes bibliographical references.

    1. Slavery--History. 2. Slavery--Saint Kitts and Nevis--History.
3. Slaves. 4. Sierra Leone--History. I. Koroma, Morlai. II. Title.

HT867 .C43 2008
306.3/62--dc22   0801

Printed in the United States of America.

*F*OREWORD

Beyond the Legacy of Slavery is the living testimony of the great-grandson of a slave who survived the transatlantic Middle Passage slave trade from Sierra Leone to St. Christopher (St. Kitts). The author was born in the era of the plantocracy with its social and economic evils of abject poverty and wretchedness. As a boy he toiled, with his grandparents and parents, in the sugar cane and cotton fields at Bourkes Estate in Sandy Point.

At the completion of his primary education at the Sandy Point Boys' Primary School, he was determined not to walk in the footsteps of his forebears. He entered the motor mechanic apprenticeship scheme at the St. Kitts Basseterre Sugar Factory. He later migrated to Harlem in New York City to improve his social and economic conditions.

By the grace of God, he went above and beyond the legacy of slavery. He was able to overcome insuperable mountains of affliction, discrimination, segregation, obstruction and oppression to become a soldier, lawyer, diplomat and minister. His homecoming to Makeni, Sierra Leone, the land of his ancestral home, was one of providence, glory, triumph, freedom and unity with the ancestors.

This story and its photographs depicts his welcome, his initiation ceremony into the Temne family, with the rituals, traditional dress, change of name and celebration.

$\mathcal{P}$REFACE

The Abolition of the Slave Trade Act, which made it illegal to trade slaves throughout the British Empire and banned British ships from involvement in the slave trade, was passed by the British Parliament on March 25, 1807. In this bicentennial year of 2007, the legacy of slavery is universal and is present everywhere. The unprecedented institution of slavery tragically produced and is still producing victims of racism, racial discrimination, injustice, prejudice, suffering, oppression, segregation and brutality. The historical legacy of slavery and colonialism negatively impact Blacks in the African disapora and globally.

The descendants of African slaves must face the dilemma of this legacy. We must engage in open and frank dialogue on the issues of the legacy of slavery. We must combat, conquer and eradicate the evils of slavery and colonialism. We must take charge of our social, economical and political destiny in the development of our societies.

Morlai Koroma

INTRODUCTION

I have known Bertram L. Charles for a number of years, and during that time he has been an honest, dedicated, thoughtful and sacrificing person. He thinks very little of self and always helps when he can. At times I have pointed out to him that politics is not his line because he does not possess the ruthlessness of politicians and that he would be more suited to be a man of the cloth due to his inner self. Whereas others accumulate material things to show they have arrived, Bertram gives away instead.

After leaving the U.S. Army and pursuing studies in law, he was sensitive to the needs of ordinary people, foregoing the accumulation of personal wealth.

He served as a member of the Federation of St. Kitts and Nevis government and did not seek election again, although it was assured that he would succeed.

His intense and long work hours presented medical problems, some of which he still suffers today.

He is Pan-African and Afro-Caribbean and has made a number of trips to West Africa searching for his ancestral roots. On one of his pilgrimages, he was initiated into the Temne ethnic group of Sierra Leone, the homeland of his maternal ancestry. Hopefully those who read this book will learn a lot, pass it on and perhaps kindle a spark for justice, equality and fairness, all of which are greatly lacking today.

C.B. Mike

*B*EYOND THE *L*EGACY OF *S*LAVERY

*S*lavery is defined as the ownership, buying and selling of human beings for the purpose of forced and unpaid labor for commercial gain. From about the mid fifteenth century to the early nineteenth century, between 20 and 28 million Black Africans were brutally removed from the African Continent. They were shipped in appalling conditions to the Caribbean and the Americas and sold into slavery. Never before in the history of mankind had so many people from one continent been bought and sold as merchandise and transported to the Americas and the Caribbean against their will.

The onset of this African holocaust began with Christopher Columbus in 1492, on the rediscovery of the so-called New World. He was seeking wealth for himself and for Queen Isabella and King Ferdinand of Spain. Spain and Portugal quickly occupied the New World and needed cheap labor to work on their established plantations of sugar, cotton and tobacco. They sought wealth for their kingdoms and the global expansion of their empires. During the four-thousand-mile voyage from Africa across the Atlantic Ocean to the Caribbean and to the Americas (the infamous Middle Passage), about six million slaves perished from disease, dysentery, small pox, overcrowding, suffocation, melancholy and sheer misery. Some threw themselves overboard into the ocean, choosing rather to drown or to be devoured by sharks than to be taken from their homeland into slavery.

> *"Sharks are invariable outriders of all slave ships crossing the Atlantic, systematically trotting along-side, to be handy in case a parcel is to be carried anywhere, or a dead slave to be decently buried...."*
> —*Moby Dick,* Herman Melville[1]

Rebellious slaves were tortured by having their arms and legs cut off. They were flogged with cat-o'-nine-tails. They were imprisoned in dungeons in the hulls of the slave ships.

Soon after Spain and Portugal's penetration into the Caribbean and the Americas, Great Britain, France, the Netherlands and other European countries entered the horrific transatlantic slave market and competed with the Spanish and the Portuguese for a share of the profits from the slave trade.

In the course of his second voyage on November 12, 1493, Christopher Columbus sighted an island in the Lesser Antilles. He named the Island Sant Jago or San Cristobal after his patron, Saint Christopher, and after his own name. The island was inhabited by the Kalinago or Carib Indians. They called the Island Liamuiga ("fertile island") because of its fertile soil, abundance of fresh water, plant life and large salt ponds.

The introduction of the British dominance in the slave trade started in 1562. In this year, Sir John Hawkins, a sixteenth-century English shipbuilder, merchant, pirate and slave trader, captured natives of Sierra Leone and sold them in the Caribbean. Two of his slave ships were identified by the names of *Jesus of Lubeck* and *The Grace of God*. Certainly, God's grace had absolutely nothing to do with enslaved humans being chained together or jammed in the hull of overcrowded slave ships with no room to move in their cruel and crushing conditions. In his time, Sir John Hawkins—like so many people now—justified slavery, aggression and evil in the name of God. Many assert that slavery had and has no basis in the law of nature because it is derived from custom. Jesus Christ said:

> *"Therefore all things whatsoever ye would that*
> *men should do to you, do ye even so to them: for*
> *this is the law and the prophets" (Matthew 7:12).*

St. Paul predicates that God made the world and all things therein, that He gives "to all life, and breath, and all things, and has made of one blood all nations of men for to dwell on all the face of the earth" (Acts 17:26). Slavery is never justified. It is a crime against humanity. As such, slavers should be punished for their abominable conduct. In the transatlantic slave trade, the British were the biggest participants, followed by the French and the Dutch.

The British colonization in the Caribbean was launched in 1623, when Sir Thomas Warner, an English captain, stepped ashore at Sandy Point, St. Christopher (also called St. Kitts) after visiting other islands in the Lesser Antilles. Sir Thomas, his family and his crew decided that St. Kitts was the best place to establish a British colony due to its strategic location, its ideal position for extension in the Leeward Islands, its fertile soil, its ashy loam favorable to the sugar cane and its abundance of water. St. Kitts officially became a British colony in 1624, after Sir Thomas made peace with the indigenous Caribs and their Chief Ouboutou Tegremante. Shortly after, however, the European colonists massacred two thousand Caribs at Bloody Point in 1626.

St. Kitts, known as the Mother Colony of the West Indies, served as the base for the expansion of British colonization in the Caribbean as follows: Barbados, 1627; Nevis, 1628; Antigua and Montserrat, 1632; Anguilla, 1650; Jamaica, 1655; and Tortola, 1672.

The tobacco and cotton crops were originally the major commodities in St. Kitts. But with North America's dominance of the tobacco industry and the local low profit margins, the St. Kitts slave owners switched from tobacco production to sugar production. As a result of this shift, starting in 1640, African slaves were imported in larger numbers to provide labor for the sugar industry. In 1713, St. Kitts was a leader in sugar production in the Caribbean. By 1776, it became the richest British colony in the Caribbean per capita, and it kept that status until the late nineteenth century despite innumerable skirmishes with the French, including the battle of St. Kitts at Brimstone Hill, Sandy Point. Four hundred years after slavery, emancipation and independence, St. Kitts' golden age of sugar production came to an end on July 22, 2005.

The life of a slave was one of unbearable conditions, wretchedness, brutality, harshness and rape. Some chose to die rather than to be enslaved. Death was considered a welcome release. Under the intolerable yoke of oppression and tyranny, slaves continued their rebellion and struggle to be liberated. Escaping to the mountains or fighting guerrilla battles against the slave owners were other weapons in the struggle for freedom, in cases like St. Kitts Marcus of the bush and Jamaica Maroons. In the harbor of St. Kitts in 1737, there was a mass suicide attempt by slaves aboard the slave ship *Prince of Orange,* under the command of Captain Japhet Bird. One hundred slaves jumped overboard in the water. Thirty three were saved.

The dilemma of slaves in general—and particularly of the slaves in St. Kitts—is best described by Clement Caines, a nineteenth-century St. Kitts lawyer and a manager of eight estates of one thousand slaves:

> *"The mind that is heroic cannot fail to be generous. The Negro is generous to excess. He bestows on others not only what he wants himself but what he can hardly do without; inborn generosity and friendliness of the largest section of the slaves, the descendants of the slaves. That this should be so has always seemed to me perfectly incredible, but so I have always found it to be. I think it of interest that the inborn generosity of the West African*

*should have survived, not in the Middle Passage
merely, but centuries of exploitation and abuse,
followed by centuries of hostility, neglect, injustice...good natured and very civil."*

Summing up the fate of the Africans in the sugar lands,
Caines continued:

*"This devoted race became, therefore, the slaves
of toil in the hands of the cultivator, the slaves of
pomp in the hands of the vain, the slaves of lust in
the hands of the concupiscent, the slaves of caprice
and whim in the hands of everybody."²*

During the years 1736–1755, the condition of the slaves
was more severe than in previous years. Nevertheless, extraor-
dinary slaves, through much industry, bought their freedom,
in spite of the brutal cruelty and barbarity practiced upon
them with impunity. One such ex-slave was Olaudah Equiano
or Gustavus Vasa, an Ibo from Nigeria, benevolent slaver,
seaman, merchant, writer, explorer (Caribbean, Americas,
Britain, North Pole) and abolitionist. Equiano's eye-witness
attestations list some of the implements of torture used by the
slavers and applied to the slaves for the slightest misdemeanor:
neck yokes, collars, chains, handcuffs, leg bolts, drags, thumb
screws, iron muzzles, cats, scourges and coffins. Equiano
describes his attempt to rescue his friend, John Annis, who left
St. Kitts with the consent of his master. Annis became a cook
on a ship en route to England. His former master revoked the
consent and kidnapped Annis back to St. Kitts. When Annis
arrived in St. Kitts, he was customarily staked to the ground

with four pins through a cord, two on his wrists and two on his ankles. He was cut and flogged most unmercifully, with irons about the neck. Annis remained in this state until death relieved him from the hands of tyrants.

Equiano also reveals that it was common in several islands, particularly in St. Kitts, for slaves to be branded with the initial letters of their master's name or to have a load of heavy iron hooks hung about their necks. They were beaten or tortured, sometimes for the most trifling mistakes. Equiano narrates a spectacle in which a slave was beaten until some of his bones were broken, simply for letting a pot boil over. "Is it surprising that usage like this should drive the poor creatures to despair, and make them seek a refuge in death from these evils which render their lives intolerable?" commiserated the abolitionist. He relates how the wretched field slaves, after toiling all day for an unfeeling owner who gives them little victuals, sometimes spend their few moments of rest to gather some small portion of grass, tie it up in parcels of bits (six pence) and take it to the market for sale. Occasionally, the overseers would take the grass from them without paying for it.

Equiano points out the case of Emanuel Sankey, a Montserrat slave, who endeavored to escape his miserable bondage of slavery by stowing away on a London ship. He was discovered while the ship was under sail and he was returned to his master. His master immediately pinned Sankey to the ground by his wrists and ankles, lit some sticks of sealing wax and dripped the wax all over his back. Equiano remarks that other slaves witnessed this and other unmerciful and dehumanized acts as well, "with shuddering horror pale, and eyes aghast, They view their lamentable lot and find no rest."[3]

Thirty pieces of silver (about twenty-five pounds), as paid to Judas for his treachery of Jesus, was the amount needed to purchase a common slave. Olaudah Equiano paid seventy pounds for his manumission. The text of his manumission demonstrates the absolute power and dominion of the slave master over the slave:

> Montserrat. – To all men unto whom these presents shall come: I Robert King, of the parish of St. Anthony, in the said island, merchant, send greeting: Know ye, that I the aforesaid Robert King, for, and in consideration of the sum of seventy pounds current money of the said island, to me in hand paid, and to the intent that a negro man slave, named Gustavus Vasa, shall and may become free, have manumitted, emancipated, enfranchised, and set free, the aforesaid negro man slave, named Gustavus Vasa, for ever; hereby giving, granting, and releasing unto him, the said Gustavus Vasa, all right, title, dominion, sovereignty, and property, which, as lord and master over the aforesaid Gustavus Vasa, I have had, or which I now have, or by any means whatsoever I may or can hereafter possibly have over him the aforesaid negro, for ever. In witness whereof I the above said Robert King, have unto these presents set my hand and seal, this tenth day of July, in the year of our Lord one thousand and seven hundred and sixty-six. Robert King. Signed sealed and delivered in the presence of Terry Legay, Montserrat, Registered the within manumission, at full length, this eleventh day of July, 1766, in liber D. Terry Legay, Register.

Olaudah Equiano expressed his sentiment on this memorable occasion:

> *"I was a slave in the morning, trembling at the will of another, and before night, I became my own master and completely free. I thought this was the happiest day I had ever experienced; and my joy was still heightened by the blessings and prayers of the sable race, particularly the aged, to whom my heart had ever been attached with reverence."*[4]

John Newton, former slave trader, converted preacher, poet and abolitionist (retrospectively), opined "that the condition of slaves were wretched in the extreme." The converted John Newton authored his testimony in the lasting hymns "How Sweet the Name of Jesus Sounds" and "Amazing Grace."

> *Amazing grace how sweet the sound,*
> *That saved a wretch like me,*
> *I once was lost, but now am found;*
> *Was blind, but now I see.*
>
> *'Twas grace that taught my heart to fear,*
> *And grace my fears relieved.*
> *How precious did that grace appear,*
> *The hour I first believed.*
>
> *Thro' many dangers, toils and snares,*
> *I have already come.*
> *'Tis grace that brought me safe thus far,*
> *And grace will lead me home.*

When we've been there ten thousand years,
Bright shining as the sun,
We've no less days to sing God's praise,
Than when we first begun.

The hellish and torturous treatment of slaves motivated John Newton to personally investigate their treatment in St. Kitts and Antigua in 1755. His fact-finding inquiry resulted in the Consolidated Slave Act of 1784, which, among other stipulations, abolished cruel and severe punishments, regulated slaves' working hours, their clothing, their spare time and the length of their meals, and exempted from all labor female slaves who had borne six children. This ameliorative law was the precursor to the Abolition of the Slave Trade Act in 1807, the Emancipation Act of 1833, and the prohibition of slavery in 1838.

On August 1, 1834, slavery was forever abolished and declared unlawful in St. Kitts. The continued harsh and oppressive treatment and living conditions of the freed African and Creole slaves led many to believe that emancipation was an illusion at best. The liberated slaves and offspring were still in actual slavery, contrary to their legitimate and lawful rights granted by the Emancipation Act of 1833. In order to maintain and perpetuate slavery, the former slave owners established the "plantocracy," a system in which the white plantation owners and former slave masters were now the planters, manufacturers and merchants of the sugar industry, with open support from the existing British Colonial rule. In the daily lives of the "freed" slaves, slavery was legally abolished, but freedom was not actually experienced. The plantation owners controlled the economy, enacted laws to protect their cheap labor supply for the sugar production and were the prosecutors, judges and jurors. Consequently, former slaves and their descendants were severely constrained in their options for social, political and economic improvement. The only form of education permitted during slavery (and for some time after) was the conversion of slaves offered by missionaries. The Blacks were excluded from the white establishment in the life of the plantocracy. Though free, Blacks were still living in abject poverty with slave wages and miserable conditions.

At the start of the nineteenth century my ancestors were listed on a slave ship manifesto as part of the human cargo. They were packed together in chains under the hull of a slave ship. They survived the horrific transatlantic journey from West Africa through the notorious Middle Passage and across the Atlantic Ocean to the Caribbean. They ended up at the slave trade market in St. Kitts and were bought and sold as personal property. They were subjected to be gifted, inherited or bequeathed at the whims of their owner. Their final destination was Sandy Point, where they slaved in the sugar cane and cotton fields with no expectation of returning to their homeland. Like other forcibly displaced Africans, they were stripped of their culture, history, language and religion. They were required to sever all ties to their African heritage, but they preserved some of their religious rituals, crops, foods, clothing, habits, customs, skills and musical artistry from Africa.

Before the Lord formed me in the womb and before I was born, the Lord knew me and had a plan and purpose for my life in common to all men and women. I was born April 13, 1937, in the era of the plantocracy and British colonial rule, in

Sandy Point, St. Kitts, to Olive Matilda Herbert and Reginald Charles. My family consisted of siblings, aunts, uncles cousins and grandparents. My formative years were influenced, in large part, by the adversities of the plantocracy and colonialism, with their intrinsic systemic poverty, low wages, illiteracy, wretchedness, woeful housing conditions, thatch houses, inadequate health care, scant running water, no electricity, no toilets, unpaved roads, and with little or no hope of social advancement. I was confined by the borders of the sugar cane fields all around me, from the mountain to the sea.

Approaching my boyhood years, my mother would wake me at the crowing of the cock Tuesdays to Fridays, and we would leave the house to work her daily task—cutting grass or picking and gathering sugar cane tops for fodder for the cattle and horses at Bourkes Estate. These beasts of burden were used for hauling the sugar canes from the fields to the railway siding. The canes were packed in trucks and transported by steam locomotives to the Basseterre Sugar Factory. My duty was to head the faggots of grass from the hillsides, valleys, ravines and other places unsuitable for the planting and harvesting of sugar canes, and take them to accessible roads where they would be drawn by horse carts and carried to the estate yard.

On Mondays, my job was to buy ground provision for food, particularly cassava, from small farmers. The cassava root would be processed into meal, which could be used to make cassava bread. The bread would then be sold in order to supplement our household's paltry weekly wages of two shillings and six pence (60 cents). On Saturdays, my responsibility was to go to the mountain, with other boys, and gather and head dry bundled wood. The wood was used as fuel for the three large stone fireplaces that we used for cooking in the open. Sometimes the firewood was confiscated at the whim and fancy of the estate manager only to rot in the estate yard.

During the summer, I was fully engaged in the back-breaking work of picking cotton in the scorching sun at Bourkes estate. All my daily chores had to be completed before I could leave for the Sandy Point Boys' Primary School located at The Alley, Sandy Point. I walked barefoot to school about two miles in sunshine and rain. After school I wore tattered clothing. At night the house was lighted by an oil lamp. I slept on the floor on lodgings.

The majority of the people were in the same state and condition of living as I was. We were poverty-stricken but not impoverished of food, strength, history, culture, sense of purpose, identity and ancestry. Some Black leaders—such as my boyhood heroes Thomas Manchester, a Sandy Pointer, planter, founder and first president of the St. Kitts Workers League, Ltd. (renamed the St. Kitts Nevis Labour Party), and Robert Llewellyn Bradshaw—refused to accept these deplorable societal adversities. They created mechanisms to improve the squalid and inglorious state of the masses and to fight the plantocracy and colonialism, two of the infections of the legacy of slavery, which infected every level of society.

In January of 1948, the St. Kitts Nevis Trade and Labour Union and the St. Kitts Nevis Labour Party, both under the leadership of Robert Llewellyn Bradshaw, demanded an increase of the plantation wages, shorter working hours and better working conditions for the workers in the sugar industry. The Sugar Producers Association (Planters) rejected the demands of the Union and welcomed a general strike to settle the labour dispute. The Planters vowed to starve the strikers into submission rather than offer a small wage increase to the workers. The workers endured extreme hardships and all kinds of deprivations. For most of the striking families, sugar cane was used as food for breakfast, lunch and dinner. Though famished, the strikers held strain for thirteen weeks. In the end, the calamitous general strike of 1948 revolutionized the social, economic and political landscape of St. Kitts and Nevis. As a direct result of this strike, the Labour Party won all seven electoral seats on the inception of universal adult suffrage in 1952. Blacks, the descendants of slaves, now governed St. Kitts, Nevis and Anguilla under the Premiership of the Honorable Robert L. Bradshaw, a Standard VII scholar. (St. Kitts and Nevis eventually gained independence from Great Britain on September 19, 1983.) The unique political climate and the historical landmark of adult suffrage in St. Kitts and Nevis in 1952 presaged my calling as a social engineer. In my young mind, I concluded that political power was the best mechanism to improve and uplift the lot of the poor working class. "Moreover who He did predestinate, them He also called: and whom he justified, them He also glorified" (Romans 8:30).

One other fateful event from my childhood particularly affected me. On Easter Monday of April 1950, two friends and I walked in the bright sunshine for about two miles from Mount Idle to Brimstone Hill Fortress. We joined thousands of other people converged on the citadel for the annual Easter celebration of fun and frolic. Everyone wanted to witness the featured event of the steel band clash. Among the ominous named steel bands in attendance for the competition were None Shall Escape (from Sandy Point), Hells Gate, Devil Dodgers, Desperados and Invaders. In the midst of the dancing and reveling and the clashing of the bands on the citadel, a sudden downpour of rain sparked a stampede among the frenzied revelers. My two friends and I were caught in the center of the bedlam. When the tumult ended, I was unscathed. But my two boyhood friends had been trampled to death. All in all, ten people died that day. The question of why they died and I was saved lingered with me. This traumatic episode affected my young adult years.

The St. Kitts Nevis Grammar School (high school) was established for the secondary education of the boys of the planters, the privileged and a few poor yet bright scholarship recipients. My teachers in primary school had called me bright, and I was hopeful that I might go to grammar school on scholarship. I gained two Standard VII school leaving certificates at age fourteen. It was my earnest desire to further my secondary education. Occasionally students randomly received scholarships to attend St. Kitts Nevis Grammar School. Unfortunately, I was never given the opportunity to answer the roll call at the only high school for boys in Basseterre. I continued to attend the Sandy Point Boys' Primary School but found it uninspiring, boring and frustrating. I moved to the Middle Island Primary School, a one-classroom wooden building five miles from Sandy Point. I was welcomed by the head teacher, Eunice Williams, and under her tutelage I was assigned extra lessons to advance my studies.

On leaving primary school, I determined not to walk in the footsteps of my ancestors toiling in the sugar cane and cotton fields, hewing wood or drawing water. I knew that obtaining clerical work would be very difficult because I was from Sandy Point and I did not have a high school education. I persistently sought a job at the St. Kitts Basseterre Sugar Factory, and I was finally awarded with a position as an apprentice. I was designated to the motor mechanic apprenticeship scheme, a remainder of one of the master plans of the plantation system. My younger days of waking at dawn had prepared me for my twenty-four-mile bicycle commute to and from work every day. The year was 1953, and I earned one dollar a day.

While I was learning my trade, most of my coworkers, friends and relatives migrated to England. I had planned to do likewise, but I changed my mind in the wake of discouraging letters from friends telling me of their fight against racial discrimination. Instead, my curiosity led me to explore the surrounding islands of Nevis, Anguilla, Antigua, St. Martin and the U.S. Virgin Islands.

It was in St. Thomas that I found the answer to my quest for a good education and bettering my social and economic conditions. I attended a church service there and heard a sermon taken from St. Matthew: "But seek ye first the kingdom of God, and His righteousness; and all these things shall be added unto you" (6:33). This scripture verse revealed to me that I was to diligently seek after the Gospel of the kingdom of God and His righteousness more than food, drink, clothes, shelter, education, riches, entertainment or worldly sustenance. I made my commitment to Jesus Christ and returned to St. Kitts a new creation. I was baptized at the Pilgrim Holiness Church in Basseterre on Easter Monday of 1957, exactly seven years after my escape from the cold hands of death at Brimstone Hill Fortress on the catastrophic Easter Monday of 1950. I became a member of the Pilgrim Holiness Church in Sandy Point.

After my conversion, miracles began to attend me. A woman whom I had never met but who had heard of me promised to sponsor me to reside permanently in the United States. Her name was Lillian Stapleton, and she was a St. Kitts national living in New York. In her letter to me, she enclosed a gift of ten dollars. I declined her kind invitation and referred another person in my stead because my brother had already filed a petition for my permanent resident immigrant visa to the United States. Within a month of my contact with the Stapleton family, I received my green card to become a permanent resident of the United States.

On Thursday morning, October 29, 1959, I boarded the airplane at Basseterre, St. Kitts, bound for New York. I was ecstatic. I arrived at Idlewild Airport in the cold autumn weather, and my brother and his wife met me with a winter overcoat. Their hearty greeting and the overcoat warmed my freezing body as my brother maneuvered his car through the streets from the airport to my new home at the Paul Dunbar Apartments in Harlem.

My first impression of New York City was one of shock and awe. I was shocked by the filthy streets, the poverty, the violence, the hustle and bustle of life and the nonstop, high-speed traffic. I was equally awed by the wonders of the city, with its glitter and glamour, lights, skyscrapers, subway and transportation system and the diversity of the people. I was astounded by the large concentration of Blacks in Harlem, by the number of churches, both store front and conventional. I wondered if I could readily overcome the initial cultural shock from my introduction to the real world of living in the United States of America. As a boy, I had the mistaken belief that everyone in New York was rich and that the streets were paved with gold. This myth was influenced by the influx of returning nationals and tourists who painted pictures of

America as heaven on earth. I was startled to discover that a majority of West Indians in New York lived scanty lives and held menial jobs, but I was also gratified that a number of them and their offspring were professionals, such as doctors, lawyers, judges, professors and entrepreneurs. They were also engaged in the social, economic and political development of New York City. In fact, the first Black borough president of Manhattan—the highest municipal office in New York City— was a West Indian, and the first Black to become the boss of Tammany Hall—the Democratic Party political machine that played a major role in New York City politics—was also a West Indian.

I settled in with the Parks, a family who embraced and accepted me as one of their own. It was like I had found a home away from home. The Stapleton family also extended an open invitation to their household with the words *"mi casa es su casa"* (my home is your home). I worshiped at Union Baptist Church, four blocks from my residence, was admitted to the membership and positively participated in the activities and programs of the church. I quickly adapted to my new surroundings, and I even ventured outside the limits of Harlem by riding the buses and the subway trains to other boroughs of the city. Three weeks after my arrival, I had learned my way around town and I went in search of employment.

My first job referral was to an automotive repair garage. After a short interview, the boss told me to report to work the next day with my tools. When I responded that I did not have any tools, he appeared surprised and informed me that the other mechanics would not allow me to use their equipment. He gave me two dollars for breakfast and wished me well. This was the end of my vocation as an auto mechanic.

My second job referral was in the garment district. At the end of the interview, the employer said he would notify me by telephone if I was accepted to fill the position of stock clerk or packer. "Do not call me," he added. "We will call you." I waited for the telephone call that never came. The following Monday morning, bright and early, I presented myself at his office. The boss was surprised to see me and said, "I did not call you to work." I instinctively replied, "I know that you did not call me to work, but I need a job." He called the foreman who put me to work in a sweatshop in the garment district. I had worked at the St. Kitts Basseterre Sugar Factory for EC$1.00 per day and I was now laboring for US$1.00 per hour.

In addition to my garment job, the Stapleton's son hired me to assist him in fundraising campaigns for civil rights movements and charitable organizations at the 369th Armory in Harlem. In my fervent desire to further my education, I went to Wadleigh Night High School in Harlem at the end of each working day. All of my activities were centered on church, school and work.

I belatedly registered for the draft, and the Selective Service System threatened to send me to jail for failing to register within the legal required time limit for new immigrants. And so, my secondary education was abruptly interrupted by a letter from the Selective Service System with an enclosed subway token and an order to report at 39 Whitehall Street in downtown Manhattan on Wednesday, August 30, 1961, for induction into the United States Army. In preparation for departure, my brothers and sisters from church presented a Bible to me with their names inscribed in it. The Stapletons gave me 12 dollars and their blessings. The Parks encouraged and supported me all the way. Friends, coworkers and well-wishers attended my farewell party and joked that I should not say goodbye if I wanted to return alive. It was an event mixed with joy and sadness as we speculated on the consequences of being a soldier.

I was up early and set off on my dreadful trip to 39 Whitehall Street and my induction into the military service of the United States of America. I walked to the subway station and hopped on the train bound for downtown Manhattan. I composed myself by reading Psalms 23 and 91. I arrived at the Induction Center at 8:00 A.M. After undergoing a battery of tests and inoculations that took all day to complete, we were hustled onto a bus at 5:30 P.M. Nearly three hours later we arrived at Fort Dix, New Jersey. All of a sudden, I felt like I was hit by a bomb shell as I became aware of the fact that I was now a recruit. I was hurriedly processed through the military system, complete with government-issued uniforms, equipment and combat gear to start Basic Combat Training.

While at the firing range, I was suddenly called away and driven to the command office to take the entrance exam for Officer Candidate School, even though I was not a high school graduate. Cold and unprepared, I failed the exam. I was advised to retake the exam within six months, but I never tried again. Before the end of basic training, I requested that my Military Occupation Specialty (MOS) be Chaplain Assistant. If I couldn't be a Chaplain Assistant, I wanted to be a clerk for my Advanced Individual Training (AIT). I was relegated to infantry, heavy weapons (MOS 112), and was shipped out to Fort Chaffee, Arkansas, for my AIT.

My first encounter with racial discrimination and segregation occurred on Saturday, December 9, 1961, at the Woolworth Department Store, Main Street, Fort Smith, Arkansas.

Dressed in my Class A uniform, I entered the restaurant, sat at the counter and ordered a slice of apple pie and a cup of coffee. The waitress notified me that I would only be served if I went to the "colored section" in the back of the restaurant or if I ate outside in the cold wintry afternoon. Incensed, I demanded service and stayed seated at the counter. All eyes—including those of some other soldiers—were fastened on me during the heated exchange. The local police were called, but before they arrived at the scene, I left the restaurant in an uproar and hastily took a cab to the Army post. This unforgettable experience changed my life forever. I decided that after my army service I would become a lawyer and combat discrimination, segregation and injustice of any kind.

I shined during my training, and at the end of my AIT I was awarded a certificate for the highest points made by our squad in the proficiency tests. I was transferred to Co. A, 13th Infantry, 1st Division at Fort Riley, Kansas. At Fort Riley (Custer Hill), we had continuous, day or night field training and classes in all kinds of weather. We practiced guerilla warfare, search and destroy missions, firing and screaming in rugged terrain looking for the imaginary enemy "Charlie." We had classes on Vietnam, light and heavy weaponry, ordnance demolition and survival. I was noticed by my superiors who considered me widely read and politically informed. In times of skirmishes between Blacks and whites, I was labeled a troublemaker and smart aleck. Because of this characterization, I was constantly harassed and saddled with extra details. On several occasions I was selected Colonel's orderly or supernumerary on guard mounts. As such, I did not have to pull guard duty in the cold weather. I was doing the duty of a squad leader (E-5) while my rank was that of private first class

(E-3). I was never promoted, while others who I had trained as Forward Observers (FO) and in Fire Direction Center (FDC) techniques were upgraded to E-4 and E-5. I went beyond the limit of soldiering and enrolled for educational courses from the United States Armed Forces Institute.

Intensive, long-range field training continued, with convoys through Kansas, Missouri, Kentucky, Tennessee and Georgia for maneuvers in North Carolina and South Carolina. After weeks of non-stop, live-fire, simulated warfare in the mountains and hills of the Carolinas—which we had endured going without hot meals, C-rations, showers, or regular toilets—we took a rest break near Florence, South Carolina. The Company Commander made arrangements at a motel for the troops to have showers at a reduced rate. Once more I was faced with rank discrimination and segregation when the owner of the "whites only" motel denied Blacks the use of the showers. I was infuriated by the racism within and without the military. I told the Captain that if Blacks were refused access to the shower facilities at the motel, then he should not allow whites to use the facilities either. He glibly replied that the motel was a private business and that the military had no control over its operation.

"But, sir," I argued, "You have control over the troops as to where we go for a shower. I respectfully suggest that you erect a shower point at the staging area for all soldiers."

My plea fell on deaf ears. The Whites went to the motel and the Blacks went to the shower point.

At the end of these intensive combat exercises in the Carolinas, two soldiers were killed and three others were mentally disabled.

My deployment to Germany during the Berlin crisis took me to snow-capped Wildflecken, where, during field training exercises, hot coffee would turn to ice before I could drink it. My next emplacement was the occupation of the divided city of West Berlin situated behind the Iron Curtain, deep inside communist East Germany. Berlin was called "the Cold War's front line and the flash point of the world." We were on daily alerts and in a constant state of combat readiness. We were also engage in psychological warfare, surrounded by confrontational, hostile forces. We probed the enemy defense, secured the border and patrolled and guarded Checkpoint Charlie, the Brandenburg Gate and the Berlin Wall, among other outposts. I frequently witnessed the killing of East Germans as they attempted escape to the West, and I was powerless to do anything about it.

Finally, it was *auf wiedersehen* to Germany and *willkommen* to Kansas. We returned to Fort Riley during the Cuban Missile Crisis and were put on high alert for deployment to Cuba. We demobilized on the peaceful resolution of the conflict between the United States and the Soviet Union.

On my last day at Fort Riley, Kansas, I packed my duffle bag, shook hands, said goodbye and took a taxi to the Junction City bus depot. During my militancy in the Army, I received no disciplinary action, not even an Article 15 (formal, nonjudicial punishment). At the expiration of my term of service on August 29, 1963, I obtained Certificates of Training and awards of medals, including the Armed Forces Expeditionary medal, Army occupation medal, good conduct medal, marksman, sharpshooter, expert rifle and mortar badges and an honorable discharge from the Army of the United States of America. I boarded a greyhound bus for New York and in three days I arrived at Grand Central Station in New York City.

When I reached home, I discovered that all my clothing and personal belongings had disappeared. The next day I went shopping to replace my missing clothes and household articles, then I took a well-deserved holiday to St. Kitts, Nevis and Antigua. Within a month after returning to the civilian world, I reunited with my church, returned to work at my old job and enrolled at Washington Irving Night High School.

My friends and I attended West Indian festivities—called "monkey jump up" by some Americans—to socialize and to meet home folks. There was no division among West Indians with respect to island of birth. We were all Caribbean people in the same boat, people of color subject to racial segregation and discrimination. I became a member of the Sons and Daughters of St. Christopher Society in America, Inc. (SDSC), a benevolent organization of St. Kitts nationals living in the tri-states of New York, New Jersey and Connecticut. The SDSC was established to assist needy nationals during the Depression of the '20s and '30s in the United States. The advent of Social Security and related entitlements supplanted the goals and objectives of the SDSC. As a consequence, young people and new immigrants did not join the Society. When I became a part of the SDSC, it was a dying organization comprised mainly of senior citizens. I represented the SDSC at various religious, social and political events. This opportunity to serve the SDSC exposed me to ministers, politicians and people of influence in the communities of New York City, many of whom encouraged me to reach for the stars.

With my high school diploma in sight, I was determined that neither fatigue, sleepiness or inclement weather would stop me from gaining my certificate. I received my Academic Diploma from Washington Irving Night School, thus becoming the first in my family to graduate from high school. It would be the start of many firsts in the course of my life. I spent the evening rejoicing and giving thanks to God for helping me to complete the first milestone of my education journey. The momentous occasion was not the end of my academic development; it was the beginning of the next phase of my education, which I expected to be full of challenges and opportunities.

I applied for admission to attend the Borough of Manhattan Community College (BMCC), and I was accepted as a full time student. I was enthused by the good news that I was going to college. When the excitement faded, I wondered how I would be able to finance my studies or support myself with no visible financial resources. I recalled the advice of the school counselor who had suggested that I enroll in the evening division of City College as a non-matriculated student. This would allow me to continue my daytime employment. But I decided to reject her advice because time was not on my side. I removed all doubts from my mind and relied on the promise of God, "But my God shall supply all your needs according to his riches in glory by Christ Jesus" (Philippians 4:19). On my last day at work, I said *adieu* to my coworkers, announcing that I was quitting work to attend college. Some thought that I was kidding them; others wished me luck and encouraged me to truck on. My Jewish friend told me that if I were ever short of money I could come to him, but I never took advantage of his kind offer.

The next day I was filled with anxiety at the orientation ceremony at BMCC. We were urged, among other instructions, not to work while in School. I was energized for the beginning of my studies at BMCC, but the constant concern about paying my bills led to an evening job back in the garment district. I worked double shifts during the summer breaks to finance my college education. After two years of sweat, toil and study, I graduated from BMCC with an Associate of Arts Degree. It was another milestone along my education highway.

Both Hunter College and the City College of New York (CCNY) admitted me as a full-time transfer student. I decided to attend CCNY to pursue my college studies. In order to reduce food and transportation expenses, I moved to a rat- and roach-infested apartment at Hamilton Heights, a complex within walking distance of the campus. During orientation at CCNY, speaker after speaker stressed the high academic standard of the school, urging that the tradition and excellent reputation of the college be maintained. They painted the picture of obtaining a degree as an insurmountable challenge. I was determined to make the run successful. I often walked past and found inspiration from the statue of Alexander Hamilton (Nevisian born, one of the founding fathers of the United States and first Secretary of the Treasury) on my way to and from classes.

Coming from BMCC, where the student body was about seventy 70 percent minorities, I was surprised by the conspicuous absence of a large number of Black or Hispanic students at CCNY. A few minorities were students of Search for Education, Elevation and Knowledge (SEEK), a program for economically and educationally disadvantaged students who did not have to meet the admissions standards. But the predominant ethnic groups on campus were Jews and Italians, and both groups championed their ethnicity. Sometimes I would be the only Black in passionate class discussions about race relations in the United States.

The competition at CCNY was keener than at BMCC. I was competing with students from top city high schools who were able to study in the library from sunrise to sunset while I was juggling my time between studying and working.

The 1964 summer riot in Harlem—triggered from real or rumored police brutality, urban despair and racial injustice—gave rise to the establishment of community organizations. Among these were Harlem Youth Unlimited, Associated Community Teams and Harlem Teams for Self Help. Through peaceful means, these groups strove to improve the quality of life for the residents of Harlem. They fought for jobs and for better health care, schools and housing. I secured employment at Harlem Teams for Self Help. I worked with young people who were burdened with overwhelming social ills. I tried to make a difference in their lives by tutoring them in their studies and counseling them to enter the social, economic and political mainstream of society. At CCNY I was active in the West Indian Student Association and was chairman of the communication and information committee. In the fall of 1967, the Black Onyx Society rallied against institutionalized racism at CCNY. The anti–Vietnam War student activists joined in the cause and led a boycott of classes, sit-ins and disruption of classes. The protests evolved into a violent, campus-wide strike. The city police intervened to restore law and order on campus.

On April 4, 1968, I was in class when the school radio flashed with breaking news: Dr. Martin Luther King, Jr. had been assassinated in Memphis, Tennessee. All activities came to a halt, followed by turmoil. Burning, looting and rioting erupted in the streets. Central Harlem glowed from the flames of buildings, with the crowd chanting, "Burn, baby, burn." My mind flashed back to the riotous and rebellious summer of 1964 in Harlem. During the day, an uneasy calm ensued, but the looting and rioting continued for two chaotic nights. When a semblance of order was restored, I walked to 125th Street to survey the damage. I was amused as I passed non-Black businesses marked "soul brother" hoping to escape the looting. The signs did not prevent the plunder of the businesses; the rioters knew that the owners were suburbanites who cheated and exploited the people.

By dint of hard work, the help of others and the grace of God, I obtained my Bachelor of Arts Degree from CCNY on June 9, 1968. With my degree in hand, I passed the New York City Civil Service Social Welfare examination. I was appointed a caseworker in the Division of Education and Rehabilitation. It was the highest paid position I had ever worked.

But I did not stay for long. In short order I resigned from my job, forfeited a fellowship to pursue a Master's Degree in social work and applied to law school. I waited anxiously for news of my applications. Finally I learned that I'd been admitted to several schools, and I selected Howard University, a Black law school. On Wednesday August 28, 1968, with two suitcases in hand, I rode the subway train to the Port Authority station and boarded a greyhound bus to Washington, D.C.

It was my first trip to Washington, D.C., and I had no place to lay my head. As I pondered my plight on arrival at the bus depot, the still voice whispered in my ears, "YMCA." I took a taxi to the Young Men's Christian Association and was assigned to a drab room. I was grateful for the lodgings but disappointed by the shabbiness of the YMCA. I had expected the service to be the same as the one in Harlem. I walked to Howard University to seek housing accommodation there, and I was informed that campus dormitories were limited to undergraduates. I explored the surrounding areas for housing on my return to the YMCA, but I found nothing. The drab room would have to do.

I was in a state of ecstasy on September 3, 1968, as I paid my tuition, registered for classes, bought my text books and set off to make my run successful in law school. While liming with new students on campus, I heard someone shouting my St. Kitts nickname. I looked around and saw a boyhood friend, now a senior medical student. We greeted each other and recalled the old days growing up. As we parted, he gave me some words of encouragement, and I was heartened to see him.

Studying at the YMCA was an impossible task with the continuous noise, music and distractions of all kinds. One day walking on campus, troubled with this study impediment, I met an old friend from CCNY, another medical student. I related to him my housing predicament, and he promised to help me find a new place to live. Within two days he directed me to a vacant apartment on Fern Street in the District of Columbia. My new abode was more conducive to serious studying, and I attempted to adequately prepare myself for classes. Assignments were like Herculean tasks, with more and more required reading of cases. I quickly learned to brief cases by identifying the relevant facts and legal issues and applying the controlling principles of law in resolving each case. I avoided a lot of headaches and ulcers by studying and doing the assignments each day.

Waiting for the bus in the snow and cold for my long ride to and from school was becoming unbearable. It was clear that I needed my own transportation, both to put an end to my discomfort and for easier mobility. To that end, I procured my driver's license and bought a secondhand car in Pennsylvania while on my Christmas break. The vehicle brought me endless mechanical problems, but it served its purpose in providing my own transportation.

Unlike my undergraduate years, I was a spectator and not a participant during the tumultuous and turbulent days of boycotts and sit-ins on campus. I was fully engaged in studying and working, and I had little or no time left for extracurricular activities.

I was employed on campus by *The Journal of Negro Education*. Founded at Howard University in 1932, *The Journal* is one of the oldest, continuously published periodicals by and about Black people. While at *The Journal*, an African student from Sierra Leone joined the staff. I paid little attention to her except to speak to her in English "Creole," the tongue of the freed slaves that was forbidden to be spoken by the establishment, and to remember her name: Ada Norman. That was the extent of our acquaintanceship at Howard University, but our paths would cross again later in life.

In between my studies I held internships at the Center for Clinical Studies (CCLS) on campus, Friendship Community Center, behind the "bamboo curtain" (a Black enclave a few blocks from Capitol Hill in Southeast Washington, D.C.), the Department of Health Education and Welfare and numerous menial jobs off campus. Near the end of my studies, I interviewed for several positions, both in the private and public sectors to practice civil rights law. I was disappointed when I did not receive job offers from any of the interviewers. Both the Interstate Commerce Commission (ICC) and the U.S. Department of Labor (USDL) offered me employment, and I accepted the appointment at the USDL.

My graduation on June 5, 1971, was a mixture of joy and pensiveness. I gave praise and thanks to God and celebrated this watershed occasion with my relatives and friends. I was joyful that I completed my college and law school studies debt-free; accordingly, I was not a slave or servant to any creditor or lending institution. Since I was not indebted to any human being, I was not restricted by location in searching for employment opportunities to fulfill my primary area of legal practice and the call to serve humanity. Graduation day was also a pensive day, touched by the silence of those students who did not make it to the finish line.

On July 12, 1971, I began my employment at the Department of Labor, along with a friend and colleague from my graduating class. After the usual orientation and formalities of introductions, I was appointed as an Advisor /Attorney (GS10) in the Division of Labor Relations and Civil Rights (LR/CR) in the Office of the Solicitor (General Counsel). My position was providential in that the Lord had granted me the desire of my heart to practice law in the area of civil rights.

It was an era of widespread and entrenched racial discrimination. No industry was immune. There was discrimination in the building trades, unions, corporations, hospitality industry, restaurants and virtually every other field of employment. My earliest assignments were with the Office of the Federal Contract Compliance, which oversees the affirmative action programs and policy of Executive Order 11246, as amended (EO). The EO requires that all federal contractors and subcontractors recruit, train, plan and advance qualified ethnic minorities, women, veterans and persons with disabilities for employment. The EO also bans discrimination and requires federal contractors and subcontractors to take affirmative action to ensure that all individuals have an equal opportunity for employment, without regard to race, color, religion, sex, national origin or disability. Affirmative action was a hot button issue of the time, and in rendering my legal opinions I was guided by the principles of the rule of law, justice, equality and fairness in accordance with the mandate of the EO. In this way, I tried to implement change by my persuasive stand in support of affirmative action.

I passed the Bar exam within a year from the inception of my stint at the USDL. I was promoted to an Attorney (GS11) without an equivalent increase in pay. The USDL, through the LR/CR Division, the enforcer of the U.S. Labor Laws, became the violator of its own laws. I demanded my compensatory raise in salary, but it was deferred. I went up the chain of command to "Killjoy," my boss, but he did not affirmatively respond to my complaint. My next step was to the division of personnel. I accused Killjoy of racial prejudice and discrimination in that he had failed and refused to compensate me with my promotion in accordance with the rules and regulations of the USDL. I requested a transfer out of the LR/CR Division. Later, I was offered temporary duty in either New York or Puerto Rico. I selected Puerto Rico without hesitation.

Killjoy found himself in an untenable situation. He tried to dissuade me from going to Puerto Rico and promised my pay increase in two weeks. He described Puerto Rico as a foreign-speaking island, where no one wanted to be posted under a hard taskmaster. I looked at him with disdain and left his office. My Black colleagues urged me to stay and fight the racism and the prejudice at the USDL, but neither Killjoy, my Black colleagues nor anyone else would prevent me from going to Puerto Rico. I could not resist the divine opportunity to return to the Caribbean, another mile closer in realizing my dream. Killjoy and his surrogates had intended to hold me back through their mistreatment of me, but God used it for good in bringing my desire to pass.

I wasted no time in cleaning my desk. I delivered my car and personal belongings for storage and anxiously awaited my flight to Puerto Rico. I arrived in Puerto Rico on September 10, 1972, and I took a cab from the airport to my reserved hotel in the Condado. On my first day on the job, I had a long talk with the chief and had lunch with all the attorneys from the office. The workplace was completely different from that in Washington, D.C. The staff was like a family, working in an atmosphere of unity and tranquility. My assignments included all areas of the U.S Labor Laws that necessitated island-wide travel to the cities, towns and municipalities. I determined that Puerto Rico would be the gateway to the U.S. Virgin Islands in the course of the race set before me. A month after arriving in Puerto Rico, Washington, D.C. office advised me that my transfer was made permanent and my pay was duly increased. The next day I flew to Washington, D.C. to collect my personal property from storage, terminate my apartment lease, complete my transfer work and ship my belongings to Puerto Rico.

On March 16, 1973, I mailed my application to the U.S. Virgin Islands Committee of Bar Examiners and registered for the Bar examination scheduled for later that year. I took a fifteen-day vacation and journeyed to St. Thomas, U.S. Virgin Islands, in final preparation for the examination. On the day of the testing, I was informed that I was not qualified to take the Bar exam because I was not a resident of the U.S. Virgin

Islands. I politely asked the chairman of the Committee for
the refund of my 175-dollar registration fee, but my request
was rejected. After a war of words, I made it clear that it was
either the refund of my money or the taking of the exam. I was
permitted to take the exam, but it was evident, in my mind,
that it would be a futile exercise. I hoped that this confronta-
tion was not an omen of future roadblocks on the way toward
my goal of practicing law in the U.S. Virgin Islands.

Back from my vacation, I sent shock waves through the
office when I announced that I was quitting the job. The boss,
in his efforts to convince me to change my mind, pointed out
the benefits of staying the course: my promotion to GS12,
a salary increase and the existing assurance of employment
versus the uncertainty of making a living in the rat race. I listened carefully to his counsel but responded that no amount
of money could divert me from the purpose and plan that the
Lord had in store for me. I submitted my letter of resignation to Washington, D.C. and counted my final days at work.
In making my farewell rounds, I had lunch with colleagues
of the Federal Bar Association, a party with associates from
other divisions of the USDL and a staff dinner.

I was showered with gifts and kind farewells: *"Ay bendito"*
(Oh my God); *"que bueno"* (how beautiful); *"Dios de bendiga"*
(God bless you); *"bendiciones"* (blessings). On the last day on
the job, the boss said to me, "I will not request a replacement
for you for a period of six months, in the event that you want
to come back."

I thanked the staff for their kindness and generosity. I
gave special thanks to the boss for his counsel and offer to me.
With a heavy heart I said, *"Adios mis hermanos y mis amigos"*
(Goodbye, my brothers, sisters and my friends). How I wished

that I did not have to leave Puerto Rico, but I could not kick against the power of destiny.

I first set foot on St. Croix on November 17, 1973. I was enchanted by its beauty. It reminded me of St. Kitts' landscape and topography. The next day I attended church to give God praise and thanks for His blessings. I invoked His guidance and support as I continued on the course that would lead to the mark beyond the horizon.

I was appalled by the treatment of H-2 and H-4 certified workers, mainly from the Eastern Caribbean. I had written legal opinions on the subject of migrant workers in the United States, during my stint at the USDL, but I never envisioned the plight of lawfully bonded workers and their dependent children living in the U.S. Virgin Islands. They were denied their civil rights, were summarily deported without their belongings and denied access to the public schools. Excluding school-aged children (H-4) from attending public school was declared unconstitutional. Every Black person from the other islands of the Caribbean— regardless of immigration status or military service—was labeled "alien" by some natives and by the continentals from the United States. I could not under-stand how some people of color were practicing the very prej-udice, discrimination and bias they had experienced in the United States.

Being a veteran of the United States Army, a naturalized citizen of the United States of America and an activist in the civil rights revolution of the '60s, I had no choice but to join in the struggle for social, economic and political justice for all residents of the U.S. Virgin Islands. I was cautioned not to become involved in the activity of the United Alien Association (UAA). I ignored their warnings and joined the organization, even becoming its president. In my spare time I tutored students in Project Upward Bound, a program that prepares students of first generation, low-income families to attend college, at the St. Croix campus of the College of the Virgin Islands. I also joined the Governor's Immigration Task Force to tackle the issue of bonded workers in the U.S. Virgin Islands, and I volunteered at Legal Services of the Virgin Islands. In return, I was hired as a staff attorney.

On January 8, 1974, I was authorized by the Federal District Court to practice law before all the courts of the U.S. Virgin Islands in the representation of Legal Services. The UAA faded away in the advent of the Immigration and Naturalization Act amendments of 1975, which entitled H-2 and H-4 bonded workers to adjust their status to permanent residents of the United States of America. The apparent conflict of interest between Legal Services and my social and political activities in the community led to my resignation from Legal Services. I moved on and became an Assistant Attorney General for the Virgin Islands Department of Labor with offices in St. Croix and in St. Thomas.

The saga of my admission to the Virgin Islands Bar resumed on July 31, 1974. Once more I questioned the biased manner in which the exam was conducted and the matching of the names, numbers and seats of the candidates. I was mindful of the procedure and concluded that I was a stigmatized examinee. It was plain that passing the Bar exam was based not on merit, but on politics, favoritism, who you knew and the whims and fancies of the Committee. Accordingly, I was not surprised that I had failed the exam a second time. I requested a review of my examination to satisfy my suspicions regarding the practices of the committee in administering the exam. I was astonished by the blatant errors in the grading and computing of my papers and the method used in totaling my score on the exam. The examiner and chairman of the Committee had no answer or explanation for the invidious discriminatory action against me.

On my third try of chasing the windmills of the Committee in trying to pass the Bar, I determined that if I failed again I would take legal action against the Committee. On November 10, 1975, the secretary of the Committee of Bar Examiners notified me by letter that I had again failed to pass the Bar exam, which I had taken in July, and I requested a review of my examination. During the review, the invisible hand of God caused the examiner to unintentionally expose the examination master sheet, which revealed I had indeed passed the examination. The corrupt Committee had declared that I had failed when I had in fact succeeded. As I left the reviewer's office, I knew that I would win the war. God was now fighting my battle against the Committee of Bar Examiners for my admission to the Virgin Islands Bar.

I dispatched a complaint to the Equal Employment Opportunity Commission in Washington, D.C., alleging that the Committee of Bar Examiners' practice and pattern of administering its examinations were contrary to Title VII of the Civil Rights Act of 1964, as amended. I requested that an investigation be conducted and that the Committee of Bar Examiners grant me a passing score on the Bar examination of July 1975. The Committee invited me to a gratuitous conference that turned into an inquiry about my background, legal training and professional experience and implied that I should not take them to court. I left the ridiculous meeting resolved to take appropriate legal action forcing them to certify that I had successfully passed the Bar examination.

On February 27, 1976, I filed my discrimination complaint against the Committee of Bar Examiners in the Federal District Court of the Virgin Islands, District of St. Croix: *Bertram L. Charles, Plaintiff,* vs. *The Virgin Islands Committee of Bar Examiners, Defendants,* Civil No. 156/1976. On March 18, 1976, pursuant to the Federal Rules of Civil Procedure, I requested that the defendants, among other things, produce: any and all documents regarding the grading, reviewing, upgrading, or other evaluating of Bar examinations written or received by the defendants during 1973, 1974 and 1975; all Bar examination papers of the plaintiff submitted during 1973, 1974 and 1975; all written rules and regulations regarding the conduct, practice and evaluations of Bar examinations during 1973, 1974 and 1975.

Four days later, I received a surprise call from the Chief Judge of the District Court instructing me to meet him in his chambers. When I arrived, he explained that a compromise had been made in my case in order to avoid a public trial—as well as any adverse publicity for the legal profession or the tainting of the public image of the Committee. I was acutely aware that this was damage control. He asked if I would withdraw my complaint in return for my admittance to the Bar, and I responded that my only interest in the matter was to be admitted to the Bar. He concluded by stating that upon review I had passed the Bar examination.

On my way home, I felt no joy from what should have been a happy event in my life. It had been an unsavory experience with the Committee, to say the least. I filed my withdrawal of the complaint, followed by my application for admission to the Virgin Islands Bar. On May 5, 1976, after a brief ceremony in Court, I was admitted to the Virgin Islands Bar and to the United States Court of Appeals for the Third Circuit. More than three years had passed since my first application to sit the Bar. I shook hands with my colleagues, including the skeptics who had told me that I did not have a case against the Committee of Bar Examiners.

I transferred from the Labor Department to the Law Department and was appointed Assistant Attorney General in charge of the town of Frederiksted. On March 30, 1978, I tendered my resignation and left the Office of the Attorney General. One week later, I opened my law offices in Frederiksted for the practice of general law. After ten months of lawyering in Frederiksted, I relocated to downtown Christiansted.

I became a participating member of the Democrat Party. I established the Naturalized Citizens Association as an interest group within the Party. I dabbled into Virgin Islands politics in the general election of 1984, when no naturalized citizen stepped up to the plate to be a candidate on the St. Croix Democrat Party ticket. After I registered my name to be a candidate in the primary election, another reluctant naturalized citizen, whom I had encouraged to run, joined the race. I yielded to his candidacy, and on primary day he won.

During the heat of the general elections campaign, however, the winner of the primary withdrew from the Senate race due to lack of support. The newspaper editorials and commentaries opined that naturalized citizens were unable to be elected because of the prejudice and discrimination practiced against them. I continued organizing nationals from the respective Caribbean Islands, including the St. Kitts and Nevis United Association, into registered non-profit associations, thus laying the foundation for the election of naturalized citizens to public office. I determined to return to St. Kitts to fulfill my boyhood dream of public service in my home town. To this end, I applied and was accepted as a law student at the University of the West Indies, Hugh Wooding Law School in Trinidad. I turned over my entire law offices—including my secretary, clients, equipment and furniture—to a friend starting out in the practice of law. Some of my friends discouraged me from locating in St. Kitts but I was willing to go beyond the limits of my physical borders.

On my first trip to Trinidad, I arrived at Piarco Airport at midnight not knowing anyone or having a place to stay. I was mentally and physically prepared for such an eventuality. I hailed a taxi, and the operator happened to know me from his former residence in St. Croix. I asked him to take me to the hotel nearest the University of the West Indies at St. Augustine. He discharged me at the Ibis Hotel. Very early the next morning, I walked to the campus and secured housing at Milner Hall. Later I went to Port of Spain, purchased household furnishings and transformed my flat into a comfortable apartment, fit for adequate rest and study. I paid my school fees, bought my textbooks and hoped that this experience would be my final hurdle in the race to complete my legal studies. By God's grace I threw aside all unnecessary baggage and looked with joy toward the prize of returning to St. Kitts as a Barrister at Law and Solicitor.

Fortunately, I was not employed during the period of my studies at Hugh Wooding School of Law. Because of the anomaly, I had the opportunity to enjoy campus life and to engage in extracurricular activities. I rendered my services to the poor and needy at the Law School Legal Aid Clinic. I frequented Port of Spain and walked through Charlotte Street and Frederick Street, which sparkled memories of carnival.

I made trips to Lavantille, Belmont, Claxton Bay, Arima, San Fernando, La Brea and many other places that had fascinated me as a boy, places that I'd read about in the *West Indian Reader* and heard sung in calypsos. I took time out to visit the historical relics of the ill-fated Federation of the West Indies and the Red House and to listen to the rhetoric at Woodford Square, which reminded me of Union Square in New York City. I also traveled to Venezuela where the revolutionary spirit of the people fueled my dream to assist the underprivileged and the downtrodden.

As I was making my farewell rounds at the law school, some professors were astonished to learn that my nephew, Ronald Wilson, was also a professor. I had kept the family relationship quiet because I wanted to be judged based on my merits and not on the people I knew or family ties—the usual criteria in judging people in a class conscious society.

On the completion of my legal studies, I said goodbye to Trinidad and hello to St. Kitts. I went to Sandy Point unrecognized and stayed with my ninety-year-old mother. In the general elections of 1989, I voted for the first time in the land of my birth. I proceeded to St. Croix to give God praise and thanks for bringing me back safely from the point where I had embarked on my academic undertaking in Trinidad. I returned to St. Kitts after I learned that I was awarded the Legal Education Certificate from the Council of Legal Education, Hugh Wooding Law School, Trinidad and Tobago, West Indies. I promptly searched for a house and an office, and, in the name of Jesus, I claimed a for-sale building without money. The seller financed the purchase of the building located at Millard Street, Sandy Point, St. Kitts, and I dedicated the edifice, in perpetuity, to the service of God.

With housing and office space in order, I turned my attention to admission to the Bar. I was called to the Bars of St. Kitts and Nevis and the Organization of the Eastern Caribbean States, in the presence of my family and friends, on July 31, 1989. The historical occasion was an unequaled watershed: I was the first Kittitian licensed to practice law in the Federation of St. Kitts and Nevis and in the United States of America. Soon after my admission to the Bars, I was labeled a Labour Party lawyer. My boyhood friend, Lee Moore, former Premier of St. Kitts and Nevis, presented my application for admission to the Bars, and my longstanding associate, Sir Probyn Inniss, former Governor of St. Kitts and Nevis, seconded my application.

I opened my law offices in central Sandy Point, once the social, political, economical, commercial and financial first town of St. Kitts. It was now a blighted and neglected town. I was the only resident lawyer in my birthplace. I reestablished my law offices in St. Croix and commuted between the two islands. While I was in St. Kitts, hurricane Hugo devastated both St. Croix and St. Kitts. The house and office in St. Kitts were damaged, and the residence in St. Croix was virtually demolished. I finally closed my law offices in Christiansted and concentrated on the growth of the Sandy Point office.

I became very frustrated in practicing law before the courts. The outdated plantation and colonial statutes needed revision. In fact, the entire judicial system was in need of reform. It lacked modern legal procedure, independence of the bench, policing of the Bar, court reporting and transcription of the proceedings.

I crossed over into St. Kitts politics to seek public office, another one of my boyhood dreams. I did not need the urgings of others, such as disaffected members of the ruling Peoples Action Movement (PAM) or disenchanted supporters of the St. Kitts Nevis Labour Party (Labour Party), to enter the political fray. I accepted the invitation of the Labour Party to be its candidate for Constituency Number 5 (Sandy Point and Fig Tree) in the upcoming general elections. The Sandy Point constituency was without a leader, disorganized and in shambles. The roadway to elected office was fraught with character assassination, threats and mudslinging.

The announcement of my candidacy was greeted unfavorably by the *Democrat* newspaper, the mouthpiece of the PAM, with its policy of the personal destruction of all opposition candidates, who were perceived as enemies. The PAM slogan was, "he who is not with us is against us."

My Sandy Point maiden political speech quieted all the doubters, critics, hecklers and interrupting surrogates of the PAM. I was astounded by the telephone calls from the silent voters, congratulating and encouraging me to press on to the next general elections. I did not realize the degree of poverty that existed among the people until I entered the political arena. I gave money to some of the needy to buy bread and sugar for their hungry children and to purchase books and pencils for school. I donated toys and provided refreshments and entertainment for the children at the annual Christmas party, in gratitude to patrons who had done the same for me and other needy kids in the past. I did not count the physical and financial costs in my quest for elective office, but sought to minister and to serve the public. "Forgetting those things which are behind, and reaching forth unto those things which are before, I pressed toward the mark for the prize of the high calling of God in Christ Jesus" (Philippians 3:13-14).

On Friday, November 19, 1993, my supporters and I walked one block to the police station, paid my deposit of 150 dollars and signed the nomination papers. I was now the official Labour candidate for Constituency Number 5. The PAM minions boasted that not only would I lose but I would also forfeit my down payment by not even garnering one-eighth of the total number of votes cast on polling day. On election day of November 29, 1993, thirty-four years and one month after migrating to the United States of America, I lost the election, but I narrowed the gap which was formerly two to one in favor of the PAM in Sandy Point and Fig Tree. Three days after the general elections, no leader of the political parties was able to command the support of the majority of elected representatives to form the new government of St. Kitts and Nevis. The stalemate ended with the formation of a PAM/NRP minority coalition (5 seats) commanded by Dr. Kennedy Simmonds and a majority Labour/CCM opposition (6 seats) led by Dr. Denzil Douglas.

The installation of the new government triggered massive demonstrations in the Basseterre streets against the minority coalition administration. The protests evolved into gun fire and flames, with Labour supporters demanding new elections. St. Kitts was like a simmering volcano ready to erupt. Under pressure from the business community and the Christian Council, Simmonds succumbed to the interest groups and grudgingly pronounced that fresh elections would be held no later than November 15, 1995. Back in St. Croix, I received a visit from Douglas who urged me to run in Sandy Point. I answered the call and returned to St. Kitts. I fell ill in the heat of the political campaign, but I continued the punishing hours of glad-handing in the constituency and campaigning on the road for other Labour candidates.

When the ballots were counted on election night of July 3, 1995, Labour had gained seven out of eight seats. It was a landslide victory over the PAM in St. Kitts. I had lost again in Constituency Number 5, but this time the PAM majority was reduced to a mere 180 votes. I had turned the dynamics of St Kitts politics upside down and changed the political landscape of St. Kitts and Nevis. For this undertaking, the Labour government appointed me to the following assignments: Ambassador of St. Kitts and Nevis to Japan, South Korea and Taiwan; Alternate Delegate to the United Nations; acting Cabinet Secretary; Legal Counsel in the Ministry of Education, Labour and Social Security; and Legal Adviser in the Ministry of Foreign Affairs.

My time and effort expended in building a political power base in Sandy Point assured my place as the parliamentary representative for Constituency Number 5 in the next general elections. However, I had fulfilled my boyhood dream of serving the people. I had survived the affliction of prostate cancer in 1997 and I was sick and tired of St. Kitts and Nevis political culture. It was rank with divisiveness, tribalism, hatred, rancor, victimization, greed, selfishness and the personal destruction of opponents. So, on April 13, 1999, I informed the Prime Minister, Dr. Denzil Douglas, of my decision to retire. I was entreated to continue in the race to be the next Sandy Point elected representative, but I was not persuaded. History shows that leaders often fail to recognize when their time to go has come and their usefulness has ended, and, instead of being gloriously rewarded, they are unceremoniously thrust aside.

On Polling Day of March 6, 2000, I paved the way for the successful election of the Labour candidate for Constituency Number 5 and for the Labour Party clean sweep of all eight candidates in 2000. I was rewarded with the award of Officer of the Most Excellent Order of the British Empire (OBE) in recognition of my service to the people of St. Kitts and Nevis. I had kept the course and finished my tasks in St. Kitts. For that reason I crossed over the coastline of St. Kitts for the shores of St. Croix.

From the moment I had become a believer in Jesus Christ, studying the Word of God had an integral part in my walk of life. I had continuously participated in various religious organizations. I was Chaplain of American Legion, Post 85, Christiansted, St. Croix, U.S. Virgin Islands, chairman of the Prostate Cancer Support Group, member of the board of directors of the American Cancer Society of St. Croix and adjunct lecturer at the University of the Virgin Islands, St. Croix campus. However, I was not satisfied. I longed to go beyond my physical limits of sight and sound to something greater and richer than business as usual.

The turning point toward higher service to the Lord took place at a Methodist tent meeting. As I listened to one minister proclaim the Word of God, an urgent call flashed before my spiritual eyes: "Laborers wanted; the harvest truly is plenteous but the workers are few." The words quickened me to be a laborer in the vineyard of the Lord. I was convinced that, with God, I was capable of doing marvelous things. I communicated the revelation to the pastor, Reverend Peter J.N. Stephens. He confirmed my calling and helped me take immediate steps to fulfill my mission. At the completion of the prescribed course of studies, I was ordained a deacon and an elder by Bishop George E. Battle, Jr. of the Eastern North Carolina Episcopal District African Methodist Episcopal Zion Church. I became pastor of Medford African Methodist Episcopal Zion Church, Christiansted, St. Croix, U.S. Virgin

Islands. The Lord had qualified and equipped me, making me efficient for the work to which I was commissioned.

I was elated to put an end to the conjecture of my ancestral home. The African Genetic Ancestry certified that my DNA analysis conclusively determined that my maternal ancestry was of the Temne people in Sierra Leone and that my paternal ancestry was of the Yoruba people in Nigeria.

The Republic of Sierra Leone is located on the west coast of Africa. It is bordered by Guinea to the north and northeast, Liberia to the south and southeast and the Atlantic Ocean to the west. The capital, Freetown, was founded in 1787 as a home for repatriated freed slaves from the Caribbean, United States, Nova Scotia and Great Britain. In 1821, Sierra Leone was made the seat of government for British territories in West Africa. The Provincial capitals comprise: Bo, Southern Province; Kenema, Eastern Province; and Makeni, Northern Province. Sierra Leone obtained independence from Great Britain on April 27, 1961.

It is noteworthy that the *La Amistad* affair was directly linked to Sierra Leone. Sengbe Pieh (also known as Joseph Cinque), a Mende, was a captive slave on the *La Amistad*, a Spanish ship. On June 27, 1839, the vessel left from Havana to Puerto Principe with Sengbe and other African slaves onboard. During the journey, Sengbe Pieh unlocked his shackles and freed himself and the other slaves from their chains. They rebelled against the captain and his crew and commanded them to steer the vessel eastward to Africa. However, the crew deceived the revolters and dropped anchor off the coast of Long Island, New York. Various parties, including the owners of the slaves, filed property claims lawsuits, asserting that the slaves were their properties. They requested that the slaves be returned to them. After protracted Court hearings, the United States Supreme Court held that the Africans were free and were remanded to be released. The Mende greeted the news of the Supreme Court's decision with joy. Free at last, the ex-slaves, thirty-five man and boys and three girls, returned to Africa.

Historically, most Temnes live in northern Sierra Leone. Many are farmers, growing rice, cassava, corn, peanuts and kola for sale. Temne culture places great emphasis on individualism, hard work and personal initiative, and they have a reputation for aggressiveness. Most Yorubas dwell in southwestern Nigeria (Ibadan and Lagos). They are also farmers, growing yams, cassavas, maize and cotton. They were also engaged in fishing, crafting, blacksmithing, woodcarving, weaving and glassmaking.

The activities of slave traders along the African coast predate the discovery of the New World. From antiquity, a man could become a slave if he was taken as captive from war, sold himself into slavery or became insolvent. Nonetheless, the unprecedented institution of the transatlantic slave trade received a great boost in the latter half of the fifteenth century. It continued with the development of sugar and coffee plantations in South America and the Caribbean. Later, the demand for cheap labor increased as tobacco and cotton plantations spread to North America. The Yoruba slaves were exported from the Bight of Benin, mainly to Brazil, Cuba, Haiti, Puerto Rico and Trinidad.

The children of Israel, on their journey to the promised land, did not follow the directions of the Lord. They did not obey the order to promptly possess the land. The spies saw the enemy as giants, men of great stature and who ate up their adversaries. They perceived their own people (and themselves) as little creatures and grasshoppers. As a result of their disobedience and unbelief, an entire generation of Israelites did not enter the promised land. However, Caleb and Joshua, the two spies who reported favorably on the land, followed the Lord wholly with full purpose of heart. They exercised their faith and walked in every path of duty. They acted according to the directions of the Lord. Consequently, they entered, conquered, occupied and inherited the promised land. Like Caleb and Joshua, I also trusted the Lord in all things, thus, I was confident that the Lord would make a way for me to enter the land of my ancestors.

In hindsight, I saw that the Lord had already begun to direct my path to Sierra Leone through my previous association with the Sierra Leonean student at Howard University. Thirty-seven years later, I divinely reconnected with Ada Norman. I informed her of my lineage and of my desire to find my ancestral roots in Sierra Leone. In preparing for my search, the Lord had provided the physical, mental, spiritual and financial resources to pursue my journey to the land of my maternal ancestry. I started my pilgrimage to my motherland from St. Croix, U.S. Virgin Islands, to Texas, United States of America, to meet with Ada. Unbeknownst to me, she had postponed a planned visit to Freetown, Sierra Leone, but my itinerary was the opportune time in keeping with her revised program.

While visiting Ada in Texas, I attended an Episcopal Church in Houston, and, providentially, linked up with the parish priest, Father Johannes George, a widely known Sierra Leonean. He also was traveling to Sierra Leone. We prepared an agenda and arranged to assemble in Kenema, Sierra Leone. I reunited with Ada in London, England, and we continued to Freetown.

In Sierra Leone, I felt like I was still in the Caribbean. The local faces resembled and reflected the contour of faces of West Indians. I was fascinated by similarities in culture, language, food, taste, colors, dress, music, styles, laughter, movements and mannerisms. I soon could recognize the ethnic origin of faces in the Caribbean by the common characteristics and distinguishing features of the natives. I was reminded of my boyhood as I observed some kids playing in the streets, others plying their wares, carrying their merchandise on their heads. I, too, had done this to make ends meet in the epoch of the plantocracy.

Ada and I traveled by car, with a driver and an assistant, to the Eastern Province to join Father Johannes. During our sojourn in Kenema, we attended St. Paul's Cathedral Church, complete with a grand love feast. Unexpectedly, the team of three had a reception with Paramount Chief Alhaji Amara Benya Vangahan IV of Nongowa Chiefdom, his subchiefs and the elders at Kenema.

I continued my pilgrimage northwards to Makeni in the Northern Region of Sierra Leone. The Temnes are the founders of Makeni. As such, they are the predominant people. The Temne language is prominently spoken in the townships and the Northern District. Other ethnic groups in Makeni include the Fullas, Mandingos, Limbas, Lakos, Mendes, Susus and Creoles.

On my arrival at Makeni, the Temne heartland, I was welcomed as a special guest on a live talk show of Radio Maria. I was interviewed by broadcast and print media, including *The Exclusive Newspaper* of Freetown. Later, the delegation and I paid courtesy calls to Paramount Chiefs, subchiefs, elders, ministers, dignitaries and NGOs and conversed with the town people.

Pen could not adequately portray the events of July 19, 2006. On that monumental day, I went to the Chiefdom Headquarters. Dressed in ethnic regalia, I walked to the town square, in front of a large crowd from the community, for my initiation into the Temne ethnic group. Paramount Chief Bai Sebora Kasangha II (JP) Bombali Sebora, Makeni, presided at the initiation ceremony. The honorable Bai was ably assisted by Paramount Chief Massa Yeli Tham II (JP) Makari/Gbanti Chiefdom, Bombali District, Council of Elders, Chief Imam of Makeni, Alhaji Mohamed Lamin Koroma and Reverend Father Daniel M. Samura of the Catholic Church. The awe-inspiring ceremony commenced in English and was translated into the Krio language with Muslim and Christian prayers, followed by rituals conducted by the traditional priest: the sprinkling of libation for cleansing and honoring of the ancestors and the breaking and sharing of bread, wine and kola nuts. During the initiation, the spiritual presence of my ancestors filled the entire place. I was infused with a freedom I had never before experienced. Like the returned prodigal son, the celebration, the sprinkling of the libation, the new clothes, the shoes on my feet, the food, the traditional dress and the rituals symbolized my restored freedom and reconcil-iation with my ancestors. I was named Morlai Koroma, which means "the respected friend of God." It is the highest title that can be granted to a mortal. I was honored and humbled that my adopted name was a likeness of the qualities of Abraham, "the friend of God" (James 2:23), who is equally revered as the father of the faithful by Judaism, Islam and Christianity. At the end of the ceremony, I recalled the words of the Psalmist in Psalm 126:

When the Lord brought back the captives to Zion,
we were like those who dream. Then were our
mouths filled with laughter, and our tongues with
singing. Then they said among the nations, The
Lord has done great things for them. The Lord
has done great things for us! We are glad! Turn to
freedom our captivity and restore our fortunes,
O Lord, as the streams in the South. They who
sow in tears shall reap in joy and singing. He who
goes forth bearing seed and weeping shall doubt-
less come again with rejoicing, bringing his sheaves
with him (Psalm 126:1-6 AMP).

My journey of hundreds of miles from Freetown to the inland Provinces and back resulted in a miraculous and triumphal pilgrimage to Sierra Leone. I sensed my ancestors' presence with us in the crowd and chatter of the people. During the last leg of my journey, a friend referred to himself as a "Krio Temne" and to me as an "English Temne." The affirmation exuded a spirit of harmony and unity between the ancestors and me. It was a grand reminder that we were all members of the same kindred.

Flying over the Atlantic Ocean on my way home, I thought of the enslaved Africans who had traveled this route, four thousand torturous miles through the infamous Middle Passage. On landing once more in the Caribbean, I realized that I had completed the triangular transatlantic slave trade route: I had started the expedition from the Caribbean (St. Croix), crossed the Atlantic to Europe (England), traveled to Africa (Sierra Leone) and finished the course in the Caribbean.

I pondered anew the history of slavery. The legacy of this unparalleled institution is ubiquitous in the African diaspora as well as globally pervasive. As a direct result of slavery and its progeny (colonialism), millions of Blacks daily face racism, segregation, discrimination, injustice, inequality, oppression, cruelty and brutality. It appears that most Blacks in the diaspora are unwilling to change. They continue to live under the shadow of the past instead of taking control of their destiny and moving beyond the legacy of slavery. We must examine the present and strain forward to what lies ahead of us. Going beyond the legacy of slavery would take courage. It will not be easy to achieve our substantive goals of overcoming the adverse effects of slavery and preventing the reoccurrence of the greatest holocaust in the history of humanity. We in the diaspora must establish links to Africa in commerce, communication, investment, research, transportation, health, education and technology. In this way we can build bridges to the future socio-economic and cultural uplifting of Blacks.

Descendants of African slaves should educate their offspring about the history of Africa and slavery. They must become aware of the human misery, unbearable suffering, despair and dehumanization of the enslaved African. Blacks should teach their children this history in the home, at meal times, when they walk in the streets, when they go to the park or to the beach, when they lie down to sleep and when they rise in the morning. Every opportunity should be taken to implant the knowledge of Africa and slavery.

I have made pilgrimages to Benin, Ghana, Guinea, Nigeria, Sierra Leone and Togo. I encourage all Blacks in the diaspora to make a pilgrimage at least once in their lifetime to Africa, to be reunited physically and spiritually with the ancestors, to gain genuine freedom, forgiveness and reconciliation.

Ultimately, to eradicate the historical injustices caused by the legacy of slavery, Blacks must arise above the inherent consequences of slavery and develop initiatives for the political, social and economic empowerment of descendants of African slaves in the diaspora.

Repetition of Slavery? Never Again!

$\mathcal{A}$PPENDIX

The Emancipation Proclamation of St Kitts,
dated the seventeenth day of July eighteen hundred and thirty-four

----- "And be it further Enacted that subject to the obligations by Law imposed upon Apprentice Labourers all and every the persons who on the said *first day of August one thousand eight hundred and thirty four* (August 1, 1834) shall be the holder in slavery in this Island (St. Kitts) shall upon and from and after the said first day of August one thousand eight hundred and thirty four become and be to all intents and purposes free and discharged of and from all and all manner of slavery and shall be absolutely and forever manumitted and that the children thereafter to be born to any such persons and the offspring of such children shall in like manner be free from their birth and that from and after the said first day of August one thousand eight hundred and thirty four slavery shall be and is hereby utterly and forever abolished and declared unlawful within this Island (St. Kitts)."

PHOTOGRAPHS

Paramount Chief Bai Seroba Kansangha II, Bombali, Sebora and author

(left to right) Chief Iman, Alhaji Mohammed Lamin Koroma, PC Massa Yeli Tham II, PC Bai Sebora Kasangha II, author and Ada

Ceremony

Initiation

Ritual

Witnesses

PC Massa Yeli Tham II, Makari/Gbanti

(left to right) Fr. George, author, Rev. Fr. Daniel M. Samura, Roman Catholic Church, Makeni

Bombali District Council

Students at White Ribbon Training and Vocational Institute, Freetown, Sierra Leone

PC Alhaji Amara Benya Vangahan IV, Nongowa Chiefdom and Elders, Kenema

Maroon Church, Freetown, Sierra Leone

Brothers of Kenema, Sierra Leone

Elmina Castle, Elmina, Ghana

Male Slave Dungeon, Elmina Castle

Female Slave Dungeon, Elmina Castle

Elmina Castle, Ghana

Seller, St. Kitts

Barrister

Relay for Life

The American Cancer Society,
St. Croix Unit
greatly appreciates

Charles Bertram

For your Efforts and Dedication in the
Fight against cancer.

October 11 - 12, 2003
Date

Income Development

President

CERTIFICATE OF ANCESTRY

African Ancestry hereby certifies that

Bertram L. Charles

shares Maternal Genetic Ancestry with

the Temne people in Sierra Leone

Paramount Chief
Bai Sebora Kasangha II (JP)
Bombali Sebora, Makeni
P. C. B Kasangngsi
19/7/06

Based on a MatriClan™
analysis performed on

November 2, 2005

Rick Kittles, Ph.D.
Scientific Director

CERTIFICATE OF ANCESTRY

African Ancestry hereby certifies that

Bertram L. Charles

Shares Paternal Genetic Ancestry with

the Yoruba people in Nigeria

Based on a PatriClan™
analysis performed on

November 2, 2005

Rick Kittles, Ph.D.
Scientific Director

20

APPENDIX			
Names of Slaves 1833–1834			
Slaves in Possession			
Names	Sex	Colour	Reputed age
Jacob Davis	Male	Black	four
Isaac Bailey	Male	colored	five
John Jeoffery	Male	black	two
Little Anthony	Male	Black	thirteen
Little Billey	Male	Black	thirty nine
Little Jack	Male	Black	fifty three
Little Pompey	Male	Black	thirty eight
Martin	Male	Black	Sixty six
Mingo	Male	Black	Forty six
Nephine	Male	Black	Twenty eight
Pompey	Male	Black	Forty three
Phill	Male	Black	Twenty six
Peter	Male	Black	eighteen
Peter Bailey	Male	Colored	Three
Quashey	Male	Black	Fifty five
Robin	Male	Black	Sixty eight
Richard David	Male	Black	Twenty six
Robert	Male	Black	Twenty two
Robert Brooks	Male	Black	Thirteen
Robert Bayley	Male	Colored	Twenty one days
Sancho	Male	Black	Sixty three
Sammy	Male	Black	Fifty three
Scipio	Male	Black	Forty six
Solomon	Male	Black	Forty six

Name	Sex	Color	Age		
Rose's Jane	Female	Black	Twenty nine	Elsey	3
Belinder	Female	Black	Fifty eight	Eleanor	3
Mey	Female	Black	Forty eight	Frances	3
Sarah	Female	Black	Twenty four	Felicia	6
Sally	Female	Black	Twenty three	Frances	3
Scilla	Female	Black	Twenty two	Hester	3
Sarah Bailey	Female	Colored	Eight	Harriot	3
Sue John	Female	Black	Six	Henrietta	3
Sukey John	Female	Black	Four	Jenny	3
Abraham	Female	Black	Sixty four	Joanna	3
Charles	Female	Black	Forty eight	Jane	3
Davey	Female	Black	Forty eight	Lucy	6
Davis	Female	Black	Nine	Little Mary	2
George	Female	Black	Four	Little Catharine	3
Godfrey	Female	Black	Fifty	Little Grace	3
Henry	Female	Black	Twenty two	Little Patience	3
Joseph	Female	Colored	Twenty one	Mary Frances	3
John	Female	Colored	Seventy	Nancy	3
John Hampton	Female	Colored	Three	Nancy	3
				Patience	
Isaac	Female	Black	Seventeen	Rachel	3
				Rachall	3
Jerry	Female	Black	Thirteen	Rosey	3
John Mingo	Female	Black	Seven	Sidelia	3
Little Quaw	Female	Black	Fifty two	Sidelia	3
				Susannah	3
Little William	Male	Black	Four	Sue	3
Nat	Male	Black	Thirty	Sabina	3
Nathaniel	Male	Black	Two months	Total Two hun...	

Names of Slaves 1833–1834

ᏋNDNOTES

1. Herman Melville. *Moby Dick* (Harper & Brothers), 1851.
2. James Pope Hennessy. *The Sins of the Fathers* (London: The Trinity Press), 1967.
3. Olaudah Equiano. *The Life of Gustavus Vassa,* 1789.
4. Ibid.

SELECT BIBLIOGRAPHY

Holy Bible, King James Version

Archives, Libraries and Museums

Charles, Bertram L., *Whitehall Street*. New York: Vantage Press, 1998.

Charles, Bertram L., *All 8-2000*, Chapel Hill: Professional Press, 2001.

Charles, Bertram L., *Alien in Paradise, A Time for Healing in the U.S. Virgin Islands*. Eugene: ACW Press, 2004.

Equiano, Olaudah. *The Life of Gustavus Vassa*, 1789.

Hennessy, James Pope. *The Sins of the Fathers* (London: The Trinity Press), 1967.

Melville, Herman. *Moby Dick* (Harper & Brothers), 1851.

Thomas, Hugh, *History of the Atlantic Slave Trade*, New York, Simon and Schuster, 1997.

PUBLICATIONS
BY BERTRAM L. CHARLES

Whitehall Street. New York: Vantage Press, 1998.

All 8-2000, Chapel Hill: Professional Press, 2001.

Alien in Paradise, A Time for Healing in the U.S. Virgin Islands.
Eugene: ACW Press, 2004.

Beyond the Legacy of Slavery
Order Form
FOR DEALERS—LIBRARIES—INDIVIDUALS

Postal orders: Bertram L. Charles
P.O. Box 203
Christiansted
St. Croix
U.S. Virgin Islands 00821

Phone orders: 340-719-0075 / 332-9565

E-mail orders: mtidle@yahoo.com

Please send us the books indicated below, in accordance with your regular discounts and terms, to:

Name: _____

Address: _____

City: _____ State: _____

Zip: _____ Telephone: (_____) _____

QUANTITY	TITLE OF BOOK	RETAIL PRICE
	Beyond the Legacy of Slavery	$10.95

TRADE DISCOUNT SCHEDULE
Single or Assorted Titles
1 to 4 copies 20%
5 or more copies 40%
Libraries and institutions .10%
plus shipping and handling

If you would like to order on a consignment basis, please check here ❏

Or order from:
ACW Press • PO Box 110390 • Nashville, TN 37222
(800) 931-BOOK

or contact your local bookstore